In the Shadow of a Soldier

Standing in Faith and Knowing your Worth

V. Vample

In the Shadow of a Soldier

Standing in Faith and Knowing your Worth

V. Vample

Copyright © 2021. Valerie Vample. All rights reserved.

All rights reserved. This book or any portion thereof may not be reproduced or used in any manner whatsoever without the express written permission of the publisher except for the use of brief quotations in a book review.

To tell this story from her perspective, the author has attempted to recreate events, locales, and conversations from her memory and the memories of family members. Any resemblance to actual persons, living or dead, or actual events is purely coincidental.

Unless otherwise noted, all scriptures are KJV and are taken from the KING JAMES VERSION (KJV): KING JAMES VERSION, public domain. Printed in the United States of America

First Printing, 2021

Library of Congress Control Number: 2021914338
Hardback 978-1-951883-64-5
Paperback 978-1-951883-54-6
eBook 978-1-951883-63-8
Audio 978-1-951883-65-2

Butterfly Typeface Publishing
PO Box 56193
Little Rock, AR 72215

Dedication

I dedicate this book to all the women who have suffered physical, mental, or emotional abuse in a relationship or marriage. I want to remind you that you are worthy, and that self-love is the first step to healing. God will sustain you in every trial, but you must allow Him to lead you through it.

3 John 1:2, "Beloved, I wish above all things that thou mayest prosper and be in health, even as thy soul prospereth."

Contents

Dedication
Foreword
Acknowledgments
Introduction
Power In The Tongue 17
Chapter One
Mother Knows Best 19
Chapter Two
Life Changes 25
Chapter Three
Family 33
Chapter Four
A New Beginning 39
Chapter Five
Our First Home 45
Chapter Six
Heartbroken 49
Chapter Seven
Strangers In My Home 57
Chapter Eight
The Side Chick 63
Chapter Nine
My Affairs 69
Conclusion
Reality 79
Discussion Questions 85
About the Author 107

Foreword

As women, sometimes we tend to fall into the shadow of the one we adore most. We get caught up in pleasing everyone else and forget about taking care of ourselves. We neglect our physical, mental, emotional, and spiritual well-being. We walk in the shadow of an another (losing ourselves and never realizing we are not whole anymore), becoming only a silhouette in the dark.

V. Vample

Acknowledgments

First and foremost, I would like to thank God who has given me the courage to write and publish my story.

Next, I send my love and appreciation to my family and friends who have always been a great support system and inspiration to me.

To the ladies of the "True Believers Church," I extend much gratitude and appreciation for the "push" to get this book finished.

Thank you all!

In the Shadow of a Soldier

Introduction: Power In The Tongue
Careful What You Ask For

As a child, I grew up in a two-parent home. Things were not always perfect, but I was happy. We did not have a lot, but we had everything we needed. We were never without a roof over our heads, lights and water, clean clothes, and good food. We did not realize that we were in the lower class because my parents worked hard to make sure we had the things we needed, and some of the things we wanted.

Proverbs 18:21, "The tongue has the power of life and death, and those who love it will eat its fruit."

My parents were not high school graduates, so they felt that it would be a great accomplishment if we made it through high school. I went off to college but returned home after two weeks (for crazy reasons). My parents, not realizing the importance of education past high school, did not insist that I go back.

So, I went off to work at a shoe factory and I soon joined the dating world.

I always knew that I wanted to marry and have children. I felt as though it was meant to be.

I remember saying, "I want to marry and stay married; no matter what."

Be careful in what you ask for. There is power in the tongue!

Proverbs 18:21, "The tongue has the power of life and death, and those who love it will eat its fruit."

In the Shadow of a Soldier

Chapter One: Mother Knows Best
Warning, Danger Ahead

When I first started dating Reginald, there were clear signs of dysfunction and abuse, but I chose to ignore them. If a man's mother and sister tell you that he is crazy, believe it!

Like I said, the warning signs of danger ahead were clear and there almost from the beginning.

First, he was older. But being a romantic at heart, young, and naïve it wasn't hard for me to convince myself that someone who was more experienced was exciting instead of someone to be cautious about.

A month into our relationship, Reginald dropped a bomb on me.

"I'm married," he announced, "but I'm separated."

I was stunned but also already in love and didn't know how to do what I knew I should do, which was to run to the other way. One evening, before I had the chance to break it off with him, my sister decided to tell him that I was pregnant. She was convinced she was doing what was best for me because he was in the army and could take care of the baby.

"Is it mine?" He asked.

I hesitated to respond. By then, I think I knew that what I had been calling love was really infatuation. Something told me that having his baby meant I'd be tied to this man forever and I wasn't sure I wanted that. "Yes," I said finally.

He was so excited!

He entered perfect boyfriend mode, and there was nothing I wanted that he would not get for me (Ladies, sometimes a wolf really will disguise himself in sheep's clothing.). This man was there for me throughout everything, and so two weeks before the baby was born, I said, "Yes," again and we got married.

In the Shadow of a Soldier

It seemed to me that he loved me and wanted to make me happy. So, although all the signs early on had pointed to danger ahead, I thought our problems had become things of his past now that we were married.

"Baby, I'll never hurt you again," he said.

"I'll always take care of you," he promised.

And I believed him. We moved to an historic part of town into a big old white house which we decided to buy. We were happy. At least I thought I was.

The baby was born in November. It was a baby girl. I became a new wife and mother in all of two weeks.

Shortly after the move, my husband received orders to go TDY (temporary duty travel) to Panama for two months. We agreed it was best for me and the baby to remain behind with my parents until he returned. He decided to put our things in storage since I would be going home to live with them, but somehow a lot of my things came up missing.

V. Vample

Some of the things were from my high school days and were a great emotional loss for me. Later, when the dust cleared, I've often wondered if threw them away.

Anyway, those two months went by quickly. He returned to the states and was stationed close to home only to find out that his unit was being sent out again on a peace-keeping mission for three to six more months. I was pregnant again by then with our second child. We kept in touch by phone, letters, and pictures.

2 Timothy 2:75, "Consider what I say, and the Lord giveth thee understanding in all things."

While he was deployed, we had our first major problem as a married couple.

He was demoted from Staff Sgt. down to Sgt. I wasn't even told what happened until he got home and then I wasn't told the full story. That's when the lies began. Although the story changed several times over the years, to put it nicely, he allowed

In the Shadow of a Soldier

females to come on base for the enjoyment of the soldiers.

Proverbs 4:5, "Get wisdom, get understanding: forget it not; neither decline from the words of my mouth." Proverbs 3:5, "Trust in the Lord with all thine heart; and lean not unto own understanding." 2 Timothy 2:7, "Consider what I say, and the Lord giveth thee understanding in all things."

Chapter Two: Life Changes
The Maybes of Life

We were stationed in the Midwest. It was a beautiful place with beautiful mountains. The girls and I enjoyed it there. We had fun playing in the snow and riding cardboard boxes down the hills. We met new friends.

This will be a fresh start for us. I thought.

After about a month, Reginald started going out all the time with his friends. This is when I began to find phone numbers (many numbers) that he had left in his pockets or his "junk room." It felt like he did not even care if I saw them. At times it didn't seem he cared about me either.

One night, after he had gotten dressed his friend stopped by to pick him up.

"Honey, please stay home," I begged him. "The girls and I miss you."

He ignored me. I really wanted to be a good wife

and mother. However, it didn't seem he was ready for a real commitment.

"Please," I cried and tried to hold on to him as he headed for the door. "Don't go."

He pushed me, and I fell to the floor.

Ignoring the pain and humiliation, I grabbed his legs still begging him not to leave, but he just took his foot and kicked me off him as if I were a bug.

After that, the drinking, women, gambling, lying, and of course, the abuse (physical, verbal, and emotional) got worse. Once, he took our clothes to the barracks to wash them, and because of his all-night drinking and gambling, the next day he came home without our clothes.

"Someone stole them, I swear!"

His gambling was a major problem too. One month he gambled our money away and we did not have money for food or diapers. He fished for an entire month and that is what we ate. It took a long time before I would ever eat fish again!

In the Shadow of a Soldier

Thank God we lived on post. This meant we did not have rent or an electric bill.

But I also knew that my mama was praying for me. I knew God had a ram in the bush!

One of my husband's commander's wife befriended me. She was older than I was. Even though I tried to conceal it, she saw what I was going through. She would let me babysit a few hours a week so that I could earn money for diapers. She always tried to make me feel good about myself by allowing me to earn money. She didn't want me to view her help as a "hand out."

Psalms 46:1, "God is our refuge and strength, a very present help in trouble."

She would say, "You're helping me as much as I'm helping you."

Psalms 46:1, "God is our refuge and strength, a very present help in trouble."

V. Vample

Psalms 124:8, "Our help is in the name of the Lord, who made heaven and Earth."

One summer, Reginald's sister came to visit. She brought her toddler son with her. This particular sister-in-law had only one leg because, during pregnancy, it was discovered that she had bone and intestinal cancer. I always got along with my in-laws. They were like sisters to me. One day, when my husband was at work, my sister-in-law decided to tell me a secret that she had been keeping.

"*You have to promise me you won't tell him,*" she warned.

"*I won't,*" I agreed, eager to know the secret.

But when I found out what it was, I had to confront him. When we lived in our hometown, he had slept with her friend in our home in our children's bed.

I was hurt and disappointed, but surprisingly, I wasn't angry. All I wanted was for him to admit it and apologize. For some reason, that was important to me. Not that he wouldn't do it again, just that he

In the Shadow of a Soldier

was sorry for it.

"I didn't do that!" He said.

Instead of an apology, what I got was rage. My husband threw a large mirror down the stairs, and it shattered into pieces. He then began to attack my sister-in-law. I tried to break up the fight, but he fought me too. Frantic, I ran to my neighbor's and called the MPs (military police). They came and took him.

Maybe my sister-in-law should have kept that secret.

Maybe I shouldn't have confronted him.

Maybe my husband should have just apologized.

The next day, my sister-in-law returned home. I did not press charges for fear of hurting his military career.

Maybe that wasn't the best decision either.

It wouldn't be the last time I would have to sacrifice

myself in the name of my family. Soon after that incident, my husband began accusing me of fooling around with his friends even though I never went anywhere. I was always home with my children.

A friend once told me, "If a man starts accusing you of messing around and you know that he knows that you aren't, then he is doing what he is accusing you of doing and just trying to keep the focus off of himself."

At the time, that sounded like a whole lot of trouble and crazy nonsense to me.

But sure enough, that is exactly what Reginald was doing!

I John 4:1, "Beloved, believe not every spirit, but try the spirits whether they are of God."

2 Tim. 1:7, "For God hath not given us the spirit of fear; but of power, and of love, and of a sound mind."

I John 4:18, "There is no fear in love; but perfect love casteth out fear: because fear hath torment.

In the Shadow of a Soldier

He that feareth is not made perfect in love."

Things were very tight with our finances, so my husband was always trying to find a way to make extra money. At one point, we took in a boarder, a young soldier. This man was dating a girl in the apartments across the street who lived with her parents.

My husband had to go to the field for a week.

Even though the young man and the girl were in love, and he had always been very respectful to our home, I knew how jealous my husband was. I specifically told him that if he was going to come back and accuse me of being involved with the young soldier, then the young soldier needed to stay at the barracks.

"I trust you baby," he said, "don't you worry about a thing."

So, the young soldier stayed. When my husband returned, I was accused. That was sad, but what was sadder is he never said anything about it to the soldier. The young soldier did nothing wrong. He had always been very respectful towards me and never crossed that line, but even today, my ex-husband accuses me of that.

Besides the money the soldier was paying us to stay with us, he was also my husband's transportation. Our car had been previously repossessed.

So, the soldier was allowed to stay and had no clue that just in the other room, I was quietly enduring my husband's mental and emotional abuse.

Maybe I should have told the soldier.

Chapter Three: Family
The Happy Face

By the time we arrived at the military base in Georgia, I had silently suffered years of heart and headaches. My family had no idea. It was important to me to put on a happy face even when things were not going so great, which was most of the time.

I did not want to look the way I felt. I was still determined to make our marriage work.

The drinking got worse and so did the abuse. I was afraid of him. His rage was out of control, but afterward, he would act as if nothing happened and would be as sweet and loving as he could be.

I was on an emotional rollercoaster!

I looked in the mirror and didn't recognize the person looking back at me.

When did you become this fragile, dependent shell

of a person?

Things got rough financially, so he decided to send me and the children to my parents for a month or two. Two months became six, and he became unavailable to me and the kids. He stopped calling and stopped sending money.

My parents were taking care of us, which was unfair to them. My dad offered to pay for a divorce, but I declined his offer. I told him that he was doing enough and that I should work on it. I called my mother-in-law and told her what was going on. She advised me to call his company commander, so I did. That didn't help at all. There was still no contact and no money.

I decided to go to the Department of Social Services. When I explained my situation, my caseworker was on it! I gave her my husband's information which lit a fire under his behind.

By the weekend, Reginald pulled up to my parent's house.

In the Shadow of a Soldier

"I come to get my family," he said.

But I refused to go. He started packing our clothes anyway and I would put them back. Then he pulled a gun out from under his jacket and threatened me. My dad and mom were too old to be going through that kind of conflict. I could not put them through that after everything they had already done for me and my children, so I gave in and went back to Georgia with him. My parents never knew why I left with him.

Gal. 5:1, "Stand fast in the liberty wherewith Christ hath made us free and be not entangled again with the yoke of bondage."

When I returned to our apartment in Georgia, I quickly realized a lot of our things were missing, even the children's toys that they had gotten for Christmas only a month before we left.

One of the neighbors came over to welcome me back. She informed me that my husband came home one day and started putting things out to sell. She said that she could tell that he had been drinking. Everyone thought that I was not coming back so they purchased items from him. She had a few things that belonged to my children and offered to give them back, but I declined the offer.

Although I was back unwillingly, things did take a turn for the better.

Reginald and I decided that we needed to be in church if our marriage was to have a chance. I grew up in church, so this was nothing new to me. I became pregnant with my third child during this time. My husband gave his life to the Lord, but I did not, not then.

Romans 10:9, "That if thou shalt confess with thou mouth the Lord Jesus and believe in thine heart that God hath raised Him from the dead, thou shalt be saved."

During this time, my husband also became sick. He was sent to a medical hospital in Texas to figure out what was going on in his body. They never did diagnosis him to this day. I was back in Georgia, pregnant and caring for two small girls. I was trying

In the Shadow of a Soldier

to make things run as smoothly as possible.

When he returned home, he was saved, but not delivered. He still had outbursts of rage that I endured silence.

At the end of December, we had our third daughter, and my husband received orders to go overseas.

In the Shadow of a Soldier

Chapter Four: A New Beginning
Fixing What's Inside

Within three months, we received housing (I know it is only because he worried those people to death.). When we arrived on to the overseas military base, we saw the nicest quarters (houses), but we kept driving through. We got to another housing area, which was ours. It looked like the ghetto! I cried. The building was in much need of fresh paint. The outer door had places where the paint was missing in huge sections.

When I went inside, it was completely different. Everything was freshly painted, and it was clean. My furniture had already arrived. My husband had already placed it in the apartment. This was home for the time being. As long as I didn't go outside, I wouldn't have to look at those unpainted buildings. I soon got over it though.

I began meeting a few neighbors, and my husband introduced me to one of his buddy's

V. Vample

wives, who had two small girls. We became the best of friends and still are to this day.

After a few months, my husband had to return to the states for training. Little did I know that he had gotten an advance on his pay. He left me and the girls without money during that month. I was so upset. I decided to go see his commander so that he would send me and my children back home. I could not believe my husband would leave us far from home without any money.

Mark 16:16, "He that believeth and is baptized shall be saved; but he that believeth not shall be damned.

Luckily, there had been another friend and his wife, 20 years older than we were and wiser also. I went to her crying and told her about my plans. She said to me, "Don't go home. We will help you because if you run home, you will always run home when there is a problem." She helped me to grow up that day, and I will be forever grateful to her for that. I stayed there, and I made it through.

In the Shadow of a Soldier

When Reginald returned, things took a turn for the worse. It seemed like we were fussing and fighting all the time. I did not tell anyone, but I am sure that the neighbors heard us.

One day, my friend invited us to church. The pastor had just started his own service at a Post Chapel. This was where I gave my life to the Lord! I was also baptized there under the open heavens. It was the most rewarding and spiritual experience of my life. I will never forget it.

Mark 16:16, "He that believeth and is baptized shall be saved; but he that believeth not shall be damned."

The pastor and his wife were God-sent. Our church was small, but the members were very close. We did a lot of things together. I became very close to the first lady. We became her daughter's Godparents, and they became the Godparents of my last three.

The pastor made my husband one of his deacons because of my husband's faithfulness to our pastor and the church. Whatever the pastor needed, my husband was there to make sure that it was done. The pastor just didn't know what was going on at our home, not for a while anyway. I just kept those things inside and tried to keep a smile on my face.

Becoming a Christian does not mean that all of your problems will just go away. As a matter of fact, the enemy will do everything possible to make your life miserable so that you will turn back to him.

I Peter 5:8-9, "Be sober, be vigilant; because your adversary the devil, as a roaring lion, walketh about, seeking whom he may devour."

I also needed to be delivered. There was a spirit of worry that consumed my life, and I fought with this demon for a lot of years. I had little to no faith. I was defeated before I even started.

2 Timothy 1:7, "For God hath not given us the spirit of fear; but of power, and of love, and of a sound mind."

I did not realize what I was working with or who was working in and through me.

In the Shadow of a Soldier

I remember going to my first lady to tell her about some of the things that had been going on in my home. No matter how close we were, she would always let God lead her when ministering to me. Although she may have been upset with the situation, she always handled it in a Godly manner.

"What could you have done to make that situation turn out differently?" She asked me.

That is when I realized I had to fix what was in me and trust God for the rest. I was in no way perfect, and I had to make sure that God was pleased with me. The first thing He let me know was to shut my mouth. That was a hard test to pass. I flunked so many times, but I finally got it. Thank God!

James 1:2-4, "My brethren, count it all joy when ye fall into divers temptations: Knowing this, that the trying of your faith worketh patience. But let patience have her perfect work, that ye may be perfect and entire, wanting nothing."

After being there for some months, my husband got "set up" by one of his commanders who did not care for him, and he received a Court Marshall.

They took a stripe again, which he had made back previously, and pay.

This hurt our family tremendously.

One night, God woke me up and told me to tell him to stand still. With the prayers of the righteous, the Court Marshall was overturned.

To God be the glory!

Chapter Five: Our First Home
Going Against Authority

After being stationed back home, we decided it was time to buy a house. We purchased a three-bedroom home in a good neighborhood. A few other couples from Panama also lived in the area. All of us, except for the one couple, joined the same church. I was very close to these families; we were just like family. The other family lived only a few streets away, so our children attended the same school.

During this time, I was a homemaker for my husband and three children. I decided I wanted a job, so I started looking. I worked on post at the childcare center as the front desk clerical assistant. I soon became pregnant with my fourth child, my first and only son. People believed that my husband prayed him down from Heaven. I do not know how true that was. Before my due date, I stopped working, stayed home with the children, and took care of the home.

Proverbs 31:10, "Who can find a virtuous woman? For her price is far above rubies."

I really thought that I was an amazing mother. My husband was strict and disciplined, so I felt as though I had to make up for his unbending nature. In doing this, I became too easy. I was the one that the children would take advantage of, I later realized that my husband had gained more respect from the children than I did.

I was wrong for going against his authority. I had to admit my mistakes, and I did go to him to do so.

Ephesians 6:1, "Colossians 3:20 Children obey your parents in the Lord: for this is right."

We spent most of our time in church. Although we seemed like a happy family, there was always something going on at our home. Our house was not a happy home.

We were stationed there for a year or so before my soldier decided he wanted to go to school on a base in Kentucky. Once again, we were getting

In the Shadow of a Soldier

ready to uproot the children. We rented our house to take care of the house payments. We found a small house in Kentucky that we could afford, and the children went to a very good school. We did, however, have a hard time finding a church home, so we visited a few.

With Reginald working a lot, I was home with the children most of the time. I did meet a few friends, and I started going to one church more frequently. This was the only base I truly disliked because there was nothing to do there. I would have to drive an hour or two just to find something for the children to enjoy.

Proverbs 3:6, "In all thy ways acknowledge Him, and He shall direct thy paths."

We were there for roughly eight months when the army decided they had too many soldiers enlisted. They offered early retirement. After that situation he encountered overseas, in some way it trickled down and he was always overlooked on the E-7 list.

For this reason, he decided to take early retirement. I did not think it was a good idea with our growing family, but he chose to retire anyway.

Proverbs 3:6, "In all thy ways acknowledge Him, and He shall direct thy paths."

In the Shadow of a Soldier

Chapter Six: Heartbroken
Uncomfortable Situations

When we returned to North Carolina, our home still had renters in it, and they were going to be there another month. Our friends offered to let us stay with them. It was a tight fit, but we made it work. That was what friends did, help one another out. I was grateful for them.

Our tour with the army was over. We had to decide how we were going to take care of our family. When I mentioned to my husband that he could apply for his unemployment benefits, he refused to do it. We were getting his small retirement check, but it was not enough. He had a bright idea to start a lawn care business, and he wanted to buy a riding lawnmower.

He went looking and realized that he needed a down payment.

"Can I have your ring?" Reginald asked. "I need

V. Vample

money for the down payment."

That broke my heart. When I refused, he came over and literally took the ring off my finger! I cried like a baby. I could not believe that what I held sacred, he dismissed like it was just some random item lying around. He never went to buy it back.

We were back in the same church. No one had an idea what was going on in my home except a few of my closest friends. They never would have guessed the kind of abuse that was taking place (mostly mental and emotional, but there also was some physical). As finances became worse, so did he. He still would not apply for his unemployment benefits, which at that time were the max one could get, so it would have helped us tremendously.

> Romans 6:13, "Neither yield ye members as instruments of unrighteousness unto sin: but yield yourselves unto God..."

We were living in my husband's hometown, and his mom still lived in their family home. I got along

In the Shadow of a Soldier

great with his family. I loved them, and they loved me and our children. My mother-in-law wanted to have some work done on her house. She wanted to sign the house over to my husband so he could get a loan for the work. I told him it was not a great idea, but of course, he did it anyway.

Later, Reginald found a job doing floor maintenance in other cities, but this became a problem. The day after Christmas, we woke up to find that our van was gone. It had been repossessed! Now, we were out of a vehicle and had no transportation to go to work.

This made things worse for our family financially of course, but for me it just meant more mental and emotional strain.

My husband would borrow a neighbor's truck when he could, but one time when he could not get it, he became very physical with me. He told me that he was not going to lose his contract. He chose to walk approximately 55 miles (how crazy). As we were fighting, I was trying to get away from him. I called the police and a few friends. My friends called the pastor. My husband was locked up for 72 hours. I received a restraining order against him, so he could not come back to the house. Eventually, I caved in and let him back in.

I wanted my marriage to work, but at the time, I did not realize that I could only fix what was inside of me. I didn't understand that I could not change a person if that person did not want (or see) the need to change.

I thought I could love him into change.

Only God can change the heart, and even then, He will not force it on anyone. The person has to yield to God's will.

Romans 6:13, "Neither yield ye members as instruments of unrighteousness unto sin: but yield yourselves unto God, as those that are alive from the dead, and your members as instruments of righteousness unto God."

Things were ok for about six months. However, we became delinquent on our house note, and his

In the Shadow of a Soldier

mom was not paying hers either. It got to the point where he could only save one.

By this time, we had six children.

Most people ask, "Why did you keep having babies?"

Well, as a Christian I thought that we both should agree to stop, but my husband would not. My health started to decline with the last two pregnancies and that's when I took matters into my own hands and requested a tubulation. I had to look out for my health.

As for the houses, I told my husband that it made more sense to save ours because it was larger, and we had six children. I suggested that his mom move in with us. Needless to say, he didn't listen. We lost our home and had to move to a trailer that had many issues. Still, he got behind on the payments. I was still a stay-at-home mom because we could not afford childcare. When my youngest turned three, I did receive a job at a childcare center.

Reginald's mom later became ill and was

hospitalized. He stopped working and sat at the hospital day in and day out. I knew he loved his mom. However, he had a family to take care of, and the money I made was not enough to sustain us.

A few weeks later, his mom passed away. He didn't show his real pain because he was trying to be strong for his siblings, but it tore him apart. They did not always have the best relationship, but he loved her dearly. He forgot about the welfare of his wife and children.

After that, I had enough! I packed my things and my children's things. We took a bus to Washington State. I had friends there. My pastor and first lady from overseas urged me to come there for a new start. It was not easy bringing six children to someone else's home no matter how close we were. We made it work for a couple of months, but I wasn't comfortable living on them.

I went to get emergency service, and I began looking for a job and a place to stay that was not in a bad area. The children started school, and the younger ones were in daycare. It was still a stressful

In the Shadow of a Soldier

time for me because I was so far away from my parents and other family members. I began to feel defeated.

Someone revealed to my husband where we were, and he drove there. He surprised me, but I knew I had to get away. I checked my children out of school and daycare, and the first lady took us to a shelter. He looked for us. He followed the first lady to her job and did all kinds of crazy things. He eventually had to leave, but he did not have enough money to drive back. He had to leave the car and take a military flight back. This was a blessing for me because it gave me transportation!

A few months went by, and I hadn't found a place to live, so I decided to go back home. My husband took a plane, drove us back across the United States, and took us back to the hell I would continue to endure. I cannot blame anyone but myself though. I went back!

When we got back, things were no different. We were still behind on the rent and were eventually evicted. (The landlord padlocked the door!).

Reginald came up with the money so we could move back in. A few months later, I decided to get a job because all the children were in school except one.

One day, the landlord came to the door for the rent. We were months behind, and he wanted us out. The children were in school. I had to pack up our clothes. I placed them in the van, and we drove around until the children got out of school. We picked them up and went to my sister and brother-in-law's home (about 35 miles away). We drove back and forth every day until we found another place.

In the Shadow of a Soldier

Chapter Seven: Strangers In My Home
The Christmas Spirit

My soldier was retired now and was working at a boot camp/school for troubled teens. He really loved this job so much so that he spent more hours there than he did at home (with no extra pay). He did not realize that, in the midst of helping other people's children, he was neglecting his own, especially his son. He stayed on this job for many years, and it had a great impact on the children there. However, the result was damaging the relationship between him and his son.

As an "old school" soldier, he tried to handle his family in the same manner that he handled his recruits. The over-the-top loud voice, the strict rules, and an 'always a soldier' attitude. To compensate for his rigid behavior, I became too lenient. So, the children always came to me, and I found myself keeping secrets that I should not have kept.

After one of his graduating classes, he decided to bring one of these teenagers, a young white teen, to our house to stay. We had six children in a four-bedroom home. I did not understand my husband who was so cautious with whom he left around our children, especially since we had five girls, brought this troubled young man into our home. It was not as if he did not have anywhere to go. He had a family that was financially secured. There was no getting my husband to see things differently.

The young man stayed with us for a few months; then, he started seeing a young girl, and her parents allowed him to move in with them. He came back a few months later but only stayed a couple of days. Then, my husband took him back home to his own family. The next time we saw him, he was married with a child of his own. He called my husband sometimes to let him know how his life was going. I must admit, my husband was a great influence on those children at that school, but what about his own?

This was not the only time Reginald would bring home strangers. While living in Fayetteville, a man, off the street, started coming to our church. He did not have anything; He was really looking for

In the Shadow of a Soldier

a handout and someplace to stay for a while. Of course, my husband, being as he is, invited him to live with us. We knew nothing about this man, and I had all these daughters. I did not agree to this at all, but as per usual, what I thought did not matter.

The man slept on my couch. I was not above helping anyone because God knows that I have needed help more than a few times. However, a line must be drawn at some point (i.e., bringing a strange man into your home with your family).

James 1:19, "Wherefore my beloved brethren, let every man be swift to hear, slow to speak, slow to wrath:"

The man had not bathed in weeks or maybe months, so my chairs were ruined! I tried to take the covers off the cushions to wash them, but it was too late. He stayed a few days. My husband was trying to find work for the man, and the man soon left.

On a different occasion, I came home from work. There was a man in a bedsheet, barefoot with no undergarments on (trying to look like Jesus) in December. He was standing in my den talking to my husband. By now, my older children were in either middle or high school. He was showing his website to my husband.

Honestly, Reginald was so gullible when it came to crazy stuff! It was like all the crazy was drawn to him. He believed and bought anything. He would let anyone into our home, and he would buy crazy things, like five vending machines! One day I came home, and five vending machines were sitting in the middle of our living room floor! That was just one of the crazy things he brought home.

At this time, my husband had stopped going to church and had joined a biker club although he didn't have a bike. This was his way of getting out to party and cheat on me.

That night, he left to go to a bike party. The children and I were at home in bed asleep. Suddenly, my daughter came into my room and told me that the man with the sheet was knocking at the door. Then, he began turning the knob trying to get in.

In the Shadow of a Soldier

When that didn't work, he went to the side door trying to get inside. I quickly jumped up, grabbed a huge knife, and called the police. When the police arrived, I went to the door and explained what was going on. The man in the sheet told the police that if he didn't have anywhere to stay, he could come back here. That is what my husband had said. What foolishness is this? I told the police that my husband wasn't home, that I had my six children in the house, that the man had no underwear on, and that he was NOT coming into my home. They told him he had to leave, so he left walking down the street.

I knew he was cold, but he should not have been walking around like that in December. He was trying to catch people in the Christmas spirit.

Why would my husband even think that this was ok?

He was too busy doing his own thing. When I tried to reach him by phone, I could never get an answer. After he finally came home, I told him about it, but he acted as if he had done nothing wrong.

Things were not good at all between us. When I had to be with him, I felt like it was a chore, or I had to perform my sexual duties. There was nothing there. I was too afraid to leave because I thought I could not make it on my own with all these children. Like so many others, I stayed in the abuse. By then, it was mostly emotional and mental abuse.

James 1:19, "Wherefore my beloved brethren, let every man be swift to hear, slow to speak, slow to wrath:"

Chapter Eight: The Side Chick
Things Change

One night, I had just gotten home and was sitting in the car when my phone rang. I picked it up, but before I could say hello, I heard people talking. I soon realized it was a conversation between my husband and his good friend. Reginald was telling his friend about a lady he had met who had bought him a shirt and would do anything for him.

I sat quietly and continued to listen to the entire conversation. As soon as they finished with that conversation and started talking about something else, the phone hung up. Now, I do not know if that was Divine Intervention, but something happened to let me know what was going on.

I dialed my husband's number, told him what I'd heard and that next time he wanted to talk about another woman, he should make sure his phone was off.

V. Vample

Soon after the that, the main arrived. I searched through the phone bill until I phone a number that was coming in multiple and awkward times a day. I found it and with the help of one of my daughters, I began investigating. My daughter called the woman and pretended she was someone who had seen them together and threatened to tell his wife (me of course) and the lady begged her not to tell me.

About a day later, I called the lady. I was calm because I wanted to know everything, I mean everything to the letter. I did not raise

> *Ephesians 4:26-27, "Be ye angry, and sin not: let not the sun go down up on your wrath: Neither give place to the devil."*

my voice or anything. I asked her if she knew him and if she knew that he was married. I asked her where they usually met and if they had had sex. She said that they would meet at the Waffle House, and they did have sex. She said that she did not know that he was married until after they had had sex (that is just like a dog). I asked if they had oral sex, and she said no.

In the Shadow of a Soldier

"Reginald loves you," she said sadly. "But he's a good-looking man. Maybe we can share him. You know some women are ok with that."

She seemed to perk up at that thought and added that as long as he paid the bills, she was sure I'd be ok with it.

Little did she know, Reginald wasn't that great at paying bills. Still, I was so stunned by this!

"Baby, if my husband wants you, he can have you, but I'm not sharing," I said into the phone.

We talked a bit more and then said goodbye and hung up. Later, she called me back and asked if I had read the book, Men are from Mars. Women are from Venus? I just looked at the phone like she was crazy!

Did this side chick think we were going to be best friends now? How ironic!

I was not mad, certainly not at her. I knew my marriage was in trouble. I did not blame it all on him. I had pushed him away. I did not think I would care, but I did. I knew that I had to confront him.

About ten minutes after I had hung up the phone with the young lady, my husband pulled up. When he came in, I told him that I needed to speak with him. We went into the bedroom and closed the door. We both sat on the bed, and I began to tell him what I knew. He was in total shock! I was not raising my voice but just talking the way I would in a regular conversation. When I did this, my husband did not know what I was going to do. This made him nervous.

While we talked, his phone rang. I knew that she would try to warn him, but it was too late. He was trying to ignore it, but I said to him, "No, answer it. I know it's her."

"Don't yell at her," I said calmly. "She didn't break our marriage vows. You did."

I was so calm. I knew he was probably afraid to sleep that night.

Ephesians 4:26-27, "Be ye angry, and sin not: let

In the Shadow of a Soldier

not the sun go down up on your wrath: Neither give place to the devil."

We decided that we were going to try and work on our marriage.

For Valentine's Day, he went all out!

Reginald had a guy come to my job with gifts. He also sang me a love song! This blew all the ladies away at the daycare center. Then, when I got off work, he had a limo waiting. We went home to grab a bag, met my daughter and her husband for dinner, and spent the night at a hotel. It was nice, very nice.

Of course, things were great for a few months, but once again, things began to change.

Chapter Nine: My Affairs
Off the Pedestal

Reginald was easily frustrated and could not positively handle his stress. Instead of dealing with it on his own, he took everything out on me. In his mind, I was the reason everything went wrong in his life.

In reality, he was just not a good businessperson. By now, he had a tree-cutting business. He had gotten a loan, but instead of getting good equipment, he bought old broken-down equipment that always needed maintenance. All the money he made always went to his workers and the maintenance on those trucks.

> James 2:24, "Ye see then how that by works a man is justified, and not by faith only."

Things were bad again in our marriage. My husband was back in the church, but he still didn't see the need for us to work on things. I told him constantly that we needed to get away and take some time for ourselves if we were going to make our marriage work. He always said that he could miss church on Sunday. I kept telling him over and over, but it never happened.

I concluded that God had forgotten about me, and I was tired of waiting on Him to fix my situation. So, I said to myself, "I'm going to do me!" And that is what I did. I stopped going to church most of the time because I was not going to pretend like I was something that I was not. I knew that I could hide from people but not God. He knows everything. I was just tired of being unhappy.

My husband had gotten a contract at the company I worked for doing their floor maintenance. There were six centers in all. I thought God had forgotten about me, and I was so unhappy and tired of living the way I was living.

James 2:24, "Ye see then how that by works a man is justified, and not by faith only."

I had a measure of faith, but I did not work it. I

In the Shadow of a Soldier

could have left to get my own place, but I thought it was too hard (fear). I preferred to stay and endure the hardship. I blamed God for me not stepping out and believing in what He equipped me to do. So, that gave a devil a foot inside my door (my Christian living). My motto became "I'm going to do me!"

I was the director of a childcare facility. I had up to 15 staff members and 116 children whom I oversaw. I knew that my staff saw a change in me because I went from the conservative church lady to an Alicia Keys fan. I was singing and dancing in the office just having a good ole time. At least I thought I was.

Soon, that was not enough for me. The devil will not leave people alone until they are completely down in the dirt. I began thinking about past relationships and decided to try and locate them. The first guy I contacted was one I was crazy about almost my entire middle and high school life. We got together. We started seeing each other and calling/texting regularly. He was single. Although I was no longer in love with my husband, I was still married, and

V. Vample

I still lived in the house with him. This was totally wrong, but at that time, I did not care. I was just trying to find some happiness for myself. We hung out for a few months; then, I became bored. The devil will always make people feel unsatisfied.

Next, I contacted the man who I always felt I was connected to and should have married. He had been in the military. He was retired and was working in another state nearby. When I first contacted him, it was innocent enough. He told his wife about me (that we were friends and nothing else).

Job 20:27, "The heaven shall reveal his iniquity; and the earth shall rise up against him.

Anyway, I wrote him a letter telling him about how we broke up, how I never had closure, and how I just wanted him to know the details behind it. I really did not think that it would cause a problem, but it had. When I contacted him the next week, he told me that his wife was upset and that it would be best if we did not talk anymore. I agreed.

In the Shadow of a Soldier

Almost a year went by before I decided to contact him again. He was happy to hear from me. We began talking, and I found out that he was separated from his wife. We talked about our marital problems, and of course, this drew us closer together. We talked every day, sometimes at least five to six times, not including texting. He became so important to me to the point that I would sit on my bed while my husband watched T.V. and texted back and forth with the man. My husband never suspected anything because I was always a "goodie-to-shoes," and he had me on "some kind of pedestal." He thought that I would never fall off, but I did.

We never ran out of things to talk about; we shared things with each other that we never shared with anyone else. I really believed that this was my soulmate. We started arranging times that we could sneak away to be together. I loved him, and I knew that he loved me. The way he would gaze into my eyes, the way he stroked my hair, and the way he held me in his arms, told me that we belonged together. That was what the devil wanted me to believe, and I did.

His wife started pressuring him to come back home. She said that she would take half of his retirement if he did not although, she was retired military as well. She just wanted her man back even though he did not want her, so she used it to her advantage. It worked because he went back home, but we continued our relationship. Nothing changed between us. We continued with the secrets and lies. When people know right from wrong, but they chose wrong anyway, God will bring them to an open shame.

Job 20:27, "The heaven shall reveal his iniquity; and the earth shall rise up against him."

I decided to get a new cellphone. Not being phone savvy, I made a huge mistake. I thought once I changed my number to the new phone, all the information would be deleted. I was stupid! I left the old phone on my nightstand. One day, my husband went for something and stumbled upon my phone.

He turned it on and saw all the text messages between my friend and me. The bottom had fallen

In the Shadow of a Soldier

out! All the lies and secrecy had come to an end.

When people allow the devil to lead them into a trap, what is done in the dark will come to the light. Sin will make people think that it is ok, and the devil will always give people excuses to hide behind. I knew that I was wrong, but since I had been done wrong for so long and was so unhappy, I thought it was justified.

When I got home, Reginald jumped me and held a knife to my throat, but for some reason, I was not scared.

After that, it was all around hell! He would come to my job and call me out on what he had found. One day, he held me, hostage, in my car; the employees and parents called the police. I took out a restraining order, but it was not worth the paper it was written on.

I went back to the house to get my clothes while being escorted by the police. When I left, the police let him follow me. They only said to him "You better not follow her." He did, of course. I drove straight to my daughter's apartment, and he pulled in right behind me. I was afraid to get out of the car. My heart began to race and would not stop. I started my engine and drove myself to the hospital. He followed me there. I was too afraid to tell them I had a restraining against him because he just stood and glared at me in such anger.

"I can't believe you would treat me like this," he said.

"The thought of another man touching what's mine drives me insane," he said.

In a few days, I went back because I believed all the lies that he told me.

He wanted to know who it was because I only had initials on the phone. He told me that he had gotten a private investigator and found out who it was.

Again, I believed him, so I told on myself. To this day, I believe that he lied.

This caused major problems for the guy. My husband called the man's job to speak with the

In the Shadow of a Soldier

man's supervisor. My husband threatened to go to the man's wife to show her the texts. My husband made the man's life a living hell for a while. Of course, the man stopped communicating with me. This was very hurtful, and it took a long time for me to get over him.

That night I went to help my husband do a strip on a floor at one of the centers. He took me into one of the classrooms and slapped me around. One of my husband's friends was there (what a shell of a man) but his friend just stood outside and did nothing.

I managed to sneak away. I called my daughter and her husband. I told them what happened. They came as if they were going to help with the floor, but really, they were there to help me escape.

I went home, packed a bag, and stayed at one of my God children's homes for a couple of days.

Of course, I went back home to try to work it out.

Conclusion: Reality
Deal With Your Problems

No matter how bad the marriage or how unhappy you are, my advice is to deal with your problems and never enter into another relationship until you are free to do so. This means legally, emotionally, and spiritually.

Emotional sin is just as damaging as physical sin. Divorce doesn't necessarily mean you are ready to enter into another relationship. It takes time to heal from emotional trauma. If you don't take the time to heal, you'll only carry that pain from one relationship into the next.

> Galatians 6:7, "Be not deceived; God is not mocked: for whatsoever a man soweth, that shall he also reap."

Yes, Reginald was unfaithful but at the end of the day, when it came down to my salvation, peace, and happiness, the only indiscretions that mattered were mine.

This might sound crazy, but I am glad I got caught, not for the trouble I caused to someone else, but because I know that if I hadn't gotten caught, the inappropriate relationship would have continued.

Don't get me wrong, I do not agree with a man putting his hands on a female, but I know that I reaped what I had sown.

Galatians 6:7, "Be not deceived; God is not mocked: for whatsoever a man soweth, that shall he also reap."

Worse than letting down my family and myself, I let God down. Although, I repented and began the long journey towards getting in right standing with God, I became afraid that I would never have the closeness with Him that I one had. The connection seemed dim, but I realized that God had already forgiven me. Now I had to forgive myself.

That would take a little longer.

Repairing things with my family took work too.

In the Shadow of a Soldier

Lies and deception have a way into trickling down into the lives of the very ones we intend to love and protect. My children had, of course, suffered through all the fussing and fighting they witnessed between me and my husband.

While there were a lot of things, I managed to keep from them, they were exposed to more than any child should have ever have to witness from people who were responsible for bringing them into the world.

There were a lot of things that they did not know about, but there was enough to impact their own lives negatively.

I was always afraid that my son would follow in his father's footsteps. He and his father had a rocky relationship for years. They would fuss and fight to the point that I would have to break it up. Sometimes, I even had to leave my job to come home to break up a fight.

There are many things I regret. I could have handled things so much better. Now, my children are left with scars, even in their adult lives, that may have been prevented if I would have worked my faith.

The day the breaking point came was a day I will never forget. April 21, 2015, I packed a bag, left and never returned. On my way out, I said goodbye to my adult children and called my husband at work.

"I'm leaving," I said into the telephone receiver. "And this time, I'm not coming back."

There had been argument that day, but I'm not sure what it was about. Looking back, I know it was just the straw that broke the camel's back. I guess I had finally reached my limit. To this day, Reginald says he does not understand why I left.

But I know why.

I was an abused wife who stayed years longer than I should have. I know I'm one of the fortunate ones; many women are killed because they do not leave their abusers. Having him over my head each night until the wee hours of the morning arguing about past mistakes finally opened my eyes to the

In the Shadow of a Soldier

fact that we would never be able to get over our problems.

My divorce was finalized in January of 2017. I left everything. I gave it all up for peace of mind. With only the clothes on my back, I moved in with another one of my daughters in hopes of starting a new life.

I prayed for healing for us, and from there, a "brand new" chapter of my life began.

I am now a published author of my first children's book series. I have a bachelor's degree in theology, and I am presently working on a master's degree.

Some days I still face challenges from my past.

Things did not go as smoothly as I thought, but that is not what God promised. Some days we will have sunshine and others rain, but God will see us through them all if we allow Him to do so.

I started a new chapter in my life, a new love, and a new relationship that looks promising… but is it really?

Discussion Questions

Why do you think V. Vample married her soldier?

What are your thoughts on bringing children into a troubled marriage?

Why do you feel women continue to remain in abusive relationships?

Do you think a deeper relationship with God would have changed her situation?

Do you think that God allows trials in our lives? Why?

Will a closer relationship with God help you handle situations differently? How?

Do you think there is anything V. Vample could have done early on to change her situation? Explain your answer.

What advice would you give V. Vample in moving forward in life after divorce?

Do you think the problems V. Vample had in her marriage were due to her husband being in the military? Explain your answer?

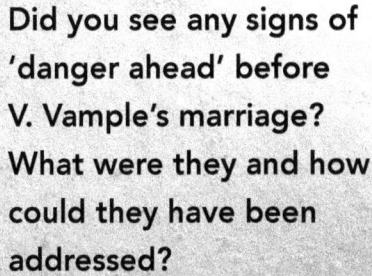
Did you see any signs of 'danger ahead' before V. Vample's marriage? What were they and how could they have been addressed?

About the Author

V. Vample spent most of her career in the education of young children. This was her passion. She served as a Preschool Administrator for over fifteen years. Later, she decided to work part-time as a substitute teacher in the Public School System.

Writing was always a passion for her even as a child. She would make up stories for her book reports and always managed to excel in them. She believes that everyone's life is a story and that there is always a lesson to be shared.

Her first book, The Big Hill, is a delightful children's book and stresses the importance of obedience in children.

The mother of six children and grandmother of eight is a native of North Carolina.

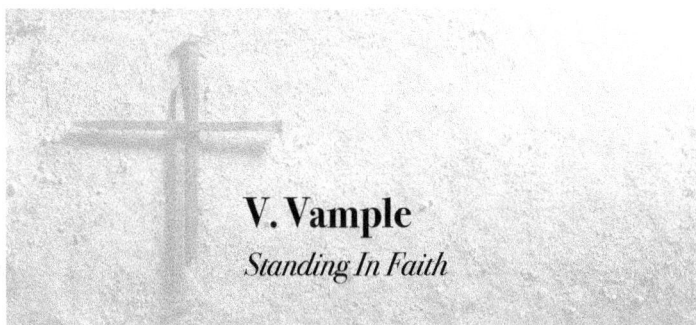

V. Vample
Standing In Faith

Sponsored By

Butterfly Typeface Publishing

Contact us for all your publishing & writing needs!

Iris M Williams

PO Box 56193

Little Rock AR 72215

www.butterflytypeface.com